Some Vernacular
Railroad Photographs

SOME
VERNACULAR
RAILROAD
PHOTOGRAPHS

Jeff Brouws and Wendy Burton

W. W. Norton & Company
New York & London

Contents

Introduction

The patina of time will transform any artifact into an object of veneration.[1]

—Sarah Greenough, *The Art of the American Snapshot*

In Praise of Vernacular Railroad Photography / Jeff Brouws

THE ACT OF COLLECTING, FOR MOST HUMAN BEINGS, seems to be encoded in our genetic makeup—a trait perhaps passed down from our hunter-gatherer origins. For me, early on, it was baseball cards and postage stamps, which I carefully stored in shoe boxes and loose-leaf albums. As a child, conceiving elaborate systems of classification—such as trying to own a card of every second baseman in the National League—was never a goal. Instead, I simply enjoyed the collecting process and the pleasures it brought. Later, as an adult, photography books became my passion; new shelves from Ikea never remained empty for long. I also began to understand that assembling collections, like the one contained between these covers, was a way to bestow order on the universe, create meaning, and temporarily control the arbitrary chaos we call life.

When I first visited the Eastern States Exposition Fairgrounds in Springfield, Massachusetts, in January 2002 to attend a railroad swap meet—forty-five years after my initial forays into collecting as a child—it wasn't surprising to feel a rekindling of familiar emotions while poring over stacks of vernacular railroad photographs: the thrill of new things to acquire, new meanings to uncover, and new orders to arrange. This is the flushed rush of excitement every collector experiences while on the hunt.

Taking place in Springfield's spacious halls was the annual Amherst Railroad Hobby show. A consortium of vendors was selling modeling items and assorted railroadiana. Portable O-, HO-, and N-gauge layouts, assembled by train clubs from around the Northeast, were also displayed. A crowd of wide-eyed rail buffs jammed the space; it was overwhelming but friendly. To get my bearings I strolled the aisles, not exactly knowing what I was there to buy but denitely on the lookout—the mind-set of a flea-market flaneur. An hour into the experience I was drawn to a booth cluttered with timetables and "railroad paper." What I hadn't known I desired was revealed: stacks of vernacular railroad photographs in plastic trays beckoned. Sorting through the piles, I began to segregate the more interesting images from those that were less so. Unearthing a few specimens of uncommon artfulness or beauty I became hooked. A new facet of my collecting life had begun.

Most of the prints were unsigned, with no identifying marks. Several had the names of their makers rubber-stamped on the back. Others, the antithesis of anonymity, contained an abundance of information faithfully recorded. Notations, inscribed on their versos in an elegant script, delineated the arcane language of locomotive wheel arrangements. Concise histories of moribund railroads were also jotted down, as so many engines were sold off from one road to another during the steam era.

Salt prints, delicate and fragile, passed through my fingers, as did the occasional cyanotype or albumen

print. Scallop- and deckle-edged snapshots—the pharmacy-produced photos from the 1930s, '40s, and '50s—were in plentiful supply. More rare were the beautiful, and more costly, razor-sharp images contact-printed on double-weight postcard stock that carried a ferrotype finish. In the main, however, single-weight silver gelatin prints made on Azo or Velox, the inexpensive Kodak papers favored by amateur photographers everywhere, formed the bulk of what I found.

And then there were the prices. Some photos went as high as five dollars, though many sold for a dollar, with the vast majority coming in at fifty cents. In this age of online auctioning, where every material object known to man has been fetishized and commodified as a "collectible"—bringing with it the fact that nothing is cheap anymore and increasingly financially out of reach for the majority of us—it was a collector's dream come true: large quantities of vernacular railroad photographs at an affordable price.

Most of what I perused in the bins were generic locomotive portraits—remnants of the International Engine Picture Club (which will come under discussion below). These images fell into two categories. The first comprised series of locomotive typologies, in which photography is useful as a tool for taxonomy (see pp. 74–75). The second type were engine studies that adhered to the strict rules of steam locomotive portraiture in vogue during the first half of the twentieth century. All shot from the same three-quarter angle, these sublime examples were made by the finest practitioners of the day, railfans of the early modern era whose names I recognized: Gerald M. Best, Fred Jukes (at right), and Mac Poor.

Sifting through the stacks, I also encountered more artistic photographs: masterful mistakes, moody exposures reminiscent of early Edward Steichen in pictorialist mode (see pp. 182–83), or pictures composed with a formal brilliance such as the little gems by H. Reid. Other images showcased the railroads' physical plant: stations, main lines, yards, roundhouses, sidings, and servicing facilities were all duly recorded. Photos of human interaction with the railroad environment were also in evidence: group portraits of crews languidly posing beside their locomotive; passengers detraining; spectators watching the "Wheels-A-Rolling" pageant at the Chicago Railroad Fair of 1948–49. One photo in particular— of a man hoisting a boy on his shoulder—was read by me as a father tenderly giving his son a glimpse of the wide world beyond the white picket fence of everyday life, a quietly poignant and archetypal image (see p. 35).

It was sheer luck that most of this "artful" material had been passed over. Thankfully, the demographic of the crowd at Springfield, with its emphasis on model railroading, did not view the photographs I was collecting in like fashion. Their intention was to use these pictures as reference material for (re-)creating scenes on prototype layouts they were building. The vendors, who viewed the pictures similarly (certainly not as collectible fine-art objects), placed no significant value on them either.

I WASN'T A NEOPHYTE TO THIS SCENE. At the time I made my first visit to Springfield I had been a photographer for thirty-five years, seventeen of them as a professional, a railfan all the while. My beginnings were humble. Appropriating the family's Kodak Instamatic at age thirteen, I made after-school forays to the local train station photographing the daily commuter trains streaming south from San Francisco. Long strings of Harriman-era coaches were the order of the day, pulled by Fairbanks-Morse H24-66 "Trainmasters." Close-to-home wanderings to shoot railroad subjects morphed into more extensive regional trips as my

teenage years unfolded. These journeys, initially conducted under parental guidance, became solo treks or buddy tours across the intermountain West after the purchase of a Volkswagen Beetle at age sixteen. Through this adolescent immersion the world of trains became an abiding passion.

Railroads have always been a subject for my camera but much of my other work as a photographer over the past two decades has involved documenting the American cultural landscape. To that end, beginning in the early 1990s and inspired by the artists Ed Ruscha and Hilla and Bernd Becher, I began compiling typologies of strip malls, tract homes, and abandoned gasoline stations (to name just a few subjects). Collecting examples ad infinitum of these cultural artifacts, I recorded the endless variety of forms available in each category. The single-minded determination brought to bear on this project not only mirrored my earlier passions for stamp and baseball card collecting but, unbeknownst to me at the time, was an activity

Photographer unknown, Wellsville, Addison & Galeton Railroad
Yard scene with boxcars and Chevrolet, Wellsville, New York,
September 1966.

Fred Jukes, Ferrocarril Central, *Engine portrait of 2-8-0 #59
at Desamparados Station,* Lima, Peru, 1934.

similar to what my predecessor railfan brethren were doing when shooting countless locomotive portraits with their postcard cameras back in the 1920s, '30s, and '40s. They, too, were compiling typologies but hadn't yet put that language to the practice.

As I looked through the thousands of images at Springfield—made by professional railfans and dedicated amateurs—I had no trouble then appreciating the motivating factors that brought these enormous archives into being, nor did I fail to understand the psychological underpinnings that drive the impassioned collector in any serious field of endeavor.

As the pace of my collecting accelerated year after year, questions arose: Who were these photographers and what led them to take the photographs that they did? What influenced the way they created them? And how did their work correlate with the overall trajectory of documentary and landscape traditions within mainstream American photography?

On the conservancy front, I also became passionately concerned about the preservation of these archives and wished to issue a "call to action,"

realizing that as collectors and railfans we need to increase awareness and ask: What will happen to those collections still out there awaiting disposition? How can we preserve them intact so as to better serve future historians and researchers delving into the mysteries of their content and biography?

All of the photographs I had acquired at Springfield, regardless of style, intention, or content, spoke these silent questions and raised important issues, eliciting in me a deep desire to unlock, explore, and ultimately protect their rich histories.

Convergence and Community

HOW DID THESE TROVES OF PHOTOGRAPHS arrive at Springfield and the other railroadiana swap meets I attended? There are outsized personalities that have had a dramatic impact on the American railroad enthusiast movement and historic turning points that have affected how it developed into what it is today. Inextricably woven into this narrative was the burgeoning field of amateur railroad photography. The growth of one parallels the other. The majority of railfans who claimed train club or historical society affiliations—even in the early modern era—used photography to document their favorite locomotives and railroads. The majority of the photographs in this book represent the fruits of their obsession, their total engagement with the hobby.

In 1917 a young locomotive engineer (and gifted photographer) on the Boston and Albany, named H. W. "Jack" Pontin, jumped onto the bandwagon. British born, he was a child who liked to paint and draw. Moving to the States in 1908, he secured a job on the railroad in 1913, studied at the Fenway School of Photography in his spare time, and built his own darkroom in 1916, honing his skills at railroad photography all the while.[2]

As a railroad employee Pontin had access to areas normally off-limits to fans. Many of his best photos— shot from engine cabs, atop water tanks or tenders— "portrayed the immediacy of railroad work."[3] Action photography of trains (as also practiced by the train

historian and photographer Lucius Beebe) was his forte and a radically different approach for the times; most fans typically made stationary locomotive portraits near depots or yards. With his growing archive he went into business and, in 1917, Railroad Photographs (later renamed Rail Photo Service) was born. It became a clearinghouse and "stock photo agency" for his images as well as the work of other train photographers he'd enlisted in the cause. Through this entrepreneurial conduit negatives and prints were sold to all factions of the rail fraternity, starting in the 1920s. Gaining notoriety, the "Railroad Photographs" byline began appearing in magazines and periodicals; by the mid- to late 1930s pictures from its extensive files were also being reproduced in seminal books such as Frederick H. Richardson and F. Nelson Blount's *Along the Iron Trail* and Beebe's *High Iron: A Book of Trains*— album-formatted, one-picture-to-a-page compendiums

of three-quarter views of fast-paced limiteds, sleek streamliners, or branchline freights, all highballing past the camera. Inclusion in these groundbreaking publications not only garnered Pontin and his bevy of staffers positive critical attention, it also announced to the world that photographing trains was an avocation shared by many.

Over the course of five decades Pontin mentored many of the nation's preeminent railroad photographers under the aegis of the RPS, offering nurturing advice on technique and camera equipment via correspondence courses and personal interaction. Through informal business arrangements with his contributing photog- raphers, he amassed a file of images covering most class-1 railroads, which in turn he offered for resale. This archive (by some estimates about 100,000 images)[4] grew to become a significant part of the print and negative trading pool that emerged, flourished, and circulated throughout the railfan community from the 1930s through the '60s. (In terms of what I found at Springfield, RPS prints represent the best of the best: Pontin's darkroom work was superb; each image was printed on double-weight postcard paper with lavish attention paid to proper contrast, burning, and dodging.)

Other important developments bringing the railfan community together happened concurrently. In 1921 Charles E. Fisher formed the Railway and Locomotive Historical Society in Boston; the National Association of Railway Enthusiasts incorporated in Boston in 1933 (instigated by Pontin); the National Railway Historical Society was founded in Baltimore, Maryland, in 1935; and the Rocky Mountain Railroad Club opened its doors in 1938.

Photographer unknown, Railroad unknown
Engine #6248 at speed with black plume of smoke
Location unknown, n.d.

Photographer unknown, Railroad unknown
Railroad enthusiasts on fantrip assembling for photo runby.
Location unknown, n.d.

As railfan organizations involved with excursions, historical research, documentation, and preservation, photography inevitably played a key role in various club activities. To wit: Pontin became one of the most admired action photographers of the day and also staged the first-known steam fan trip in 1934 for the RRE on the Hoosac Tunnel and Wilmington Railroad; and among the early members of the Rocky Mountain Railroad Club there were well-known camera-toting ferroequinologists, some who'd been "at it" since the 1910s, roaming the canyons of Colorado and the high plains of Wyoming: Otto Perry, Harvey E. High, Mac Poor, Richard H. Kindig, and Jackson Thode. Perry and Kindig both became active and faithful participants of the International Engine Picture Club.

Although there are no statistics on the number of railfans who purchased images from RPS (or the Railway Negative Exchange, another railroad photo repository operating in California),[5] or who took photographs of their own, one has to assume that photography was an important adjunct to any hobbyist pursuit. Therefore these organizations and the fraternization they encouraged, not to mention the various services creating product for the marketplace (Pontin's image bank, Beebe's books, and fan magazines), all contributed to the eventual flow of photos into swap meet venues some seventy years later.

To my mind, the biggest influence on this movement was the International Engine Picture Club, started by Freeman Hubbard, *Railroad Man's Magazine*'s humanist editor in April 1931. Hubbard presciently recognized there were people across the country interested in railroads who sought community but felt lonely and alienated in their pursuits. How better to bring them together than to form a club with a global reach (international!) and an august name, a name that gave it a ring of authority and importance? (Perhaps through its creation Hubbard, ever the worried editor, was simultaneously devising ways to boost newsstand sales and subscriptions.)

For whatever reason, this small act of creating the picture club became a foundational moment for America's railfan movement. The textual record confirms this. In *Railroad*'s "Interesting Railfan" section (a regular feature that ran monthly from April 1961 until the magazine ceased publication, in 1979), Hubbard penned homespun biographical sketches about underrecognized and well-known railroad photographers, authors, preservationists, and historians, passion being the sole criterion for inclusion in this series. Through articles written on the lives of Bert Pennypacker, Harre Demoro, Michael Koch, and others, we learn their enjoyment of railfanning was directly attributable to the International Engine Picture Club and the camaraderie it fostered. They, along with their confreres in the IEPC, rallied around the hobby, formed lifelong bonds, shared information, and exchanged negatives and prints. Through this fellowship feelings of isolation disappeared; they no longer considered themselves odd ducks or lone wolves living on the outskirts of mainstream American culture.[6]

Hubbard's own words confirm these facts, as he relates in his "Interesting Railfan no. 100" autobiographical sketch.

> There existed a section in the magazine that printed free want ads for hobbyists to facilitate the trading of negatives and prints . . . a department of the magazine that has carried on uninterrupted ever since and is now called *The Switch List*. . . . Forty years ago, readers who thought they were alone in their desire to photograph engines and trains . . . eagerly began getting in touch with other fellows having similar interests . . . That, I think, was *Railroad*'s greatest contribution to the hobby.[7]

The International Engine Picture Club in its day was analogous to contemporary social networking, with the United States Postal Service rather than the Internet acting as the delivery mechanism. Gerald M. Best, who took his first locomotive photograph in 1908, decided to start collecting locomotive portraits seriously in 1931. The timing aligns perfectly with the IEPC's debut.[8] Clearly, Best, with his wide-ranging curiosity about locomotives from around the globe, was inspired by the magazine to participate in these newly forming networks; he even bought an "ancient Graflex 3A" postcard camera to improve the quality of his work. The IEPC staged its first national photo contest in the spring of 1933 and boasted of outsized enrollment numbers 10,000-strong by the winter of 1935,[9] with all participants receiving a pin to certify their membership.[10] It even received national recognition in a *Life* magazine column entitled "Speaking of Pictures" from June 28, 1937, as the popular weekly's editors devoted three pages to steam engine photographs with captions extolling the dos and don'ts of proper locomotive portraiture, stating, "Ten years ago, interest in locomotive pictures was limited but today *Railroad Stories* (soon to become *Railroad* magazine) reports that interest is spreading fast." While it's impossible to know definitively how amateur engine pictures ended up printed in this quintessential national magazine, Hubbard may have garnered a favor from Lucius Beebe, who traveled in the same social circles as Henry Luce, *Life*'s publisher. Beebe himself would be featured on its cover a year and a half later. With *Life*'s broad circulation—some 80,000-plus subscribers and a million copies sold weekly on newsstands—this article couldn't help but boost awareness of the fledgling hobby.[11]

In an era where privacy wasn't an issue, the editors at *Railroad Stories* also printed the addresses of photographers under each published picture in the magazine to further facilitate trading. *Trains* followed suit in 1940. Enthusiasts wrote one another, purchasing prints and negatives for a nominal fee. Michael Koch, the Shay locomotive expert, recalled in a *Railroad* interview that "25 or more 616 negatives went for a dollar" and that "glass plates were the envy of many hobbyists."[12] Some entrepreneurially minded railfans did establish businesses selling images (like Pontin's Rail Photo Service), monetizing their hobby to defray expenses. But in the main most fans instigated simple bartering systems covering a wide range of activities and possibilities, negotiating "even steven" deals with one another. Money rarely changed hands.

Informal swapping (or bartering) was a keen strategy. Hard financial times during the Depression and, later, gas rationing during World War II made private car travel a luxury, so railfans—without the means to journey cross-country to take locomotive pictures of "foreign" roads (railroads geographically not close to home)—could still secure prints to round out their collections. A photographer located in Georgia might shoot six frames of postcard-size 122 film of a particular locomotive or freight car, keep one negative himself, and sell or trade the remaining five

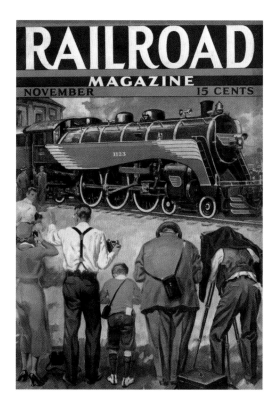

Railroad magazine cover by Emmett Watson, *entitled "On a Rail Fan Excusion," depicting train buffs taking a locomotive portrait* November 1937. Reprinted with permission from Carstens Publications. (George Cook Collection)

Gerald M. Best, Virginia & Truckee Railroad, *Portrait of 4-4-0 #22* Carson City, Nevada, n.d.

to club members in Vermont or Pennsylvania. Another locomotive shooter in California, for instance Gerald M. Best, processed film for a friend in Kentucky in exchange for engine pictures from that region. Others, as had Pontin, sometimes traded camera gear against future negatives one of his "staffers" would shoot.[13] Several photographers such as Best and Philip R. Hastings initially participated in RPS activities but for personal reasons decided not to continue on with Pontin.[14] The Hastings postcards herein (from the Jim Shaughnessy Collection), made by RPS but not distributed, are the remaining evidence of those severed ties.

The mishmash of photographs I found at Springfield, the end result of all this trading activity, were mainly without attribution. Photos and negatives circulated casually among friends, often with no expectation of remuneration or credit, so many never labeled their work. There were exceptions, however. Otto Perry placed a glass nameplate over the enlarging paper when making prints, embedding his name and address into the image to avoid questions of provenance.[15] Others, like Pontin, had a bold rubber stamp that clearly delineated an RPS "permissions" clause as well as the staff photographer's authorship, all without declaring copyright. Based on the sheer volume of many collections, it's understandable that so much of the material ended up at swap meets or on eBay as "anonymous" photographs; it would have taken a platoon of professional archivists to keep tabs on everything.

Locomotive Stills, Mainline Action, and the Snapshot: A Body of Evidence Describing Everyday Railroading

IN THE FIRST FIVE DECADES of the twentieth century, as the visual aesthetics of the field were developing, railfan photographers involved themselves in different types of image making. Principal interests that brought them to the hobby, be it transportation history, science or mechanics, scale modeling, architecture, operations, or perhaps the allure of a lonesome steam whistle wailing down the distance, informed the kinds of photos they composed or collected. Some were documentary, some were poetic, some were snapshooters. All were impassioned and obsessed, snatching any free time away from the daily toils of family and work to pursue their interests.

Predominant in number were the roster shooters, whom Lucius Beebe once referred to as the "nuts and bolts clique."[16] They took postcard-size images of engines and rolling stock with Kodak 1A, 2C, and 3A or, later, Monitor or Vigilant 616 cameras (at 2.5 x 4.25 inches the 616 negative size proportionally matches perfectly the elongated dimensions of a locomotive). Concentrating on one railroad close to home, they tried to photograph each class of engine on its roster. The favored vantage point at the time, standardized across the country, was a three-quarter view taken from the left with the side rods down, engine number, smoke box, and company name clearly showing, and preferably in flat light or strong at-your-back sunshine so that none of the drive wheel or running gear disappeared in shadow. According to the historian John H. White, pictures done this way were "undiluted by artistic interpretation" and thus pure.[17] These images ranged from casual handheld snapshots made by amateurs to a more

sophisticated approach practiced by the best lensmen using small apertures, tripods, and time exposures. All extraneous detail was excluded; telephone poles, wires, and trackside detritus were prohibited. One rail photographer, so intent on perfection, obsessively spent hours grooming his shot, ridding the roadbed beside the locomotive of distracting debris.[18]

These types of images—known as "documentary locomotive stills"—were made in locations railfans had easier access to: station platforms, yards, or roundhouse facilities. But entrée to these areas wasn't always possible. To avoid potential problems many developed long-standing relationships with railroad employees, who gave tacit approval or provided waivers granting permission to be "on the property." Gerald M. Best so ingratiated himself to roundhouse crews at Southern Pacific's Taylor yards in the 1930s and '40s he often received advance warning when a rare class of locomotive was in town; hostlers would even spot engines in the uncluttered locations he favored. Thanks to these contacts he was one of the few cameramen in Los Angeles to shoot openly around engine facilities during World War II, despite railroad installations being deemed potential military targets and thus off-limits to photography.[19]

Best also purposely concentrated on locomotive photography because he felt it a better use of his time. In an era before the advent of radio scanners (where railfans could glean dispatching information about train movements) earlier fans had to take their chances; much time was wasted along main lines waiting for trains that never arrived. Also, since the action pictures required more finesse, taking a picture of stationary objects, such as a locomotive sitting on a ready track or at rest during a station stop, guaranteed more, consistently better pictures.

A subset of fans interested in locomotive stills also collected builders' photos. The Baldwin or Alco Locomotive Works Collections with their spare, mechanistic beauty, represent the best of this kind. These builder prints with masked-out backgrounds showcased the engine's dark features, perfectly rendered against a white field (above). Professional photographers employed by the manufacturers made these images—pictures technically challenging to create. Typically the paint shop coated the left side of the engine in dark gray or flat black prior to the locomotive's official portrait; this provided more detail on the negative. Carpenters constructed white canvas backdrops to place behind the locomotives in order to facilitate further separation from the background, making it easier for in-house darkroom technicians to opaque negatives later. Finished prints—dry mounted on cardstock with the locomotive's specifications printed on the back—were approximately 3 x 8 inches (Alco) or 9 x 13 inches (Baldwin) in size. These were actual photographs and not offset lithographs. Swapping these two types of prints with fellow members of the International Engine Picture

Duane V. Bearse, Atchison, Topeka & Santa Fe Railroad *Portrait of boxcar #272900,* Location unknown, n.d.

Photographer unknown, Chicago, Aurora & DeKalb Railroad *Portrait of 4-4-0 #1 and crew,* Kaneville, Illinois, 1915–1917. (Gerald M. Best / C. P. Atherton Collection)

Photographer unknown, Indian State Railways *WP Class Baldwin streamlined 4-6-2,* location unknown, n.d.

American locomotive manufacturers. He, too, hung a large tarpaulin behind the locomotive to isolate it from the background and had engines painted in tones of gray and black to achieve maximum detail.[20]

The second major focus for rail photographers in the early era was action photos. Much more difficult to execute, these three-quarter views of trains at speed required the use of professional equipment with better lenses and faster shutter speeds. Regimented by the same strictures as those applied to roster shots, which emphasized locomotive and train detail, image makers from the action school also sought to include smoke, steam, and other suggestions of motion and speed in the frame. In fact, as the three-quarter art form evolved, with Beebe among its staunchest advocates (an advocacy that was helped along by his numerous publications), many photographers shot *only* when interesting wisps of smoke occurred or when the side rods were in their proper "down" position. Achieving such nuances became a matter of pride and skill. Most photographers used the cumbersome Graflex D, but the more sophisticated shooters, for example, Donald W. Furler and H. W. Pontin, employed larger formats (5 x 7 and 8 x 10 in Furler's case, a 4 x 5 for Pontin) to stunning effect (see pp. 136–37 and pp. 222–23). These gentlemen took their avocation seriously, stuck to Beebe's program like glue, and made work that epitomized the best of the genre. Beebe lays down his eloquent code in his book *Highliners*:

> The perfect railroad action photograph—with its rural background, its clarity of definition of all moving parts, its indication of speed through smoke and steam exhaust, its full length view of the train, and its absence of any object or matter to distract the attention from the locomotive and consists themselves—is not easy to come by. There are but a few hours each day when the flat light necessary for the clear depiction of valve motion and wheel arrangement is available, and long distances and inaccessible spots must frequently be achieved to meet these conditions.[21]

Club happened as well, with some fans amassing outsized collections. Though it's hard to pinpoint where or how this style of locomotive portraiture emerged historically, the work of John Stuart may be an important precursor. A British photographer (1831–1907) born in Glasgow, he did commissioned work for several firms, including the North British Locomotive Company, beginning in 1865. The precise and delicate craftsmanship of his albumen prints, with their stark uncluttered backgrounds, closely resemble the best images produced by

Professor George Hilton, a noted transportation historian, characterized the three-quarter-speed shot aesthetic (also known as a "wedgie" or "smoking wedge") as "the best single delineation of the emotional impact of railroading."[22] Viewed within the historical context of American railroad photography at the time, I would concur; it was a bold and technically challenging advance for the hobby.

Don Ball Jr., Chicago, Rock Island & Pacific Railroad
Freight #78 piloted by engine #5036 heads out of town
Lawrence, Kansas, December 8, 1950.

Donald W. Furler, Baltimore & Ohio Railroad
4-6-2 #5318 with the "National Limited" in tow
Jersey City, New Jersey, October 19, 1939.

Just what made the shot so difficult? It was the equipment that plagued the producer. The Graflex 3A—manufactured from 1907 to 1936 with only minor design changes—was the favored picture-making device for its day. Considered revolutionary in its time, it combined fast shutter speeds and single-lens reflex focusing. Despite these advantages, the Graflex remained a bulky view camera with a hooded eyepiece above the ground glass. It couldn't be raised to eye level; it had to be handheld at waist height or placed on a tripod, with the photographer looking down at a reversed image. Acquiring the split-second timing to photograph a moving train at speed was exceedingly difficult to do. Photographers who tripped shutters too soon wasted much film; it took months of practice to wait until it appeared the train was too near to take the shot.

Standing adjacent to the track, then, at a three-quarter angle in bright sunlight, was the easiest way to get a decent image with ASA 100 film and cameras set at f 5.6 at 1/500 second. The three-quarter view also lessened the possibility of blur—a train coming at the camera moves a smaller distance on the film plane during exposure than a train photographed from 90 degrees. Clearly, the "wedgie" wasn't as straightforward as later generations of railroad photographers derisively

assumed. A well-made photograph of a train at speed required finesse and was a rare accomplishment in 1940.

A reason many rail photographers gravitated toward action as opposed to static shots had to do with the level of harassment they received at the hands of officials while shooting around urban railroad environments (the antithesis of Gerald M. Best's experience in Southern California). Many decided it was easier to be out in the country, waiting trackside for a train to pass by, away from the gaze of authority. Otto Perry, after being arrested and questioned in Woodward, Oklahoma, during World War II by overzealous police officers who assumed he was a foreign spy, made fewer roster shots and frequented yard and roundhouse facilities less often after this experience (despite the fact he'd been obsessively shooting locomotive portraits since 1913).[23] This decision proved providential, as it drove him instead to the main lines and mountains of Colorado and Wyoming, where he created an incomparable late-career portfolio of trains at speed.[24]

WHILE I DO APPRECIATE THE BEAUTY of the three-quarter wedgie aesthetic and applaud its popularization by Beebe, I also see from a dialectical position its limitations. To my mind, trains and the landscapes they run through have a synergistic relationship; they shouldn't be photographically divorced from each other. The trackside habitat spawned by this interaction— the industrial zones, business and warehouse districts, stockyards, factories, and farmlands—is a territory shaped by social factors, historical trajectories, economics, and land use decisions. The best railroad photographs show us these relational attributes, gathering together the entire mise-en-scène. Unfortunately, during the 1920s, '30s, and '40s the acolytes of the three-quarter wedgie school missed the mark on this level. Seemingly

Photographer unknown, Pacific Electric Railway
Streetcar in urban setting, **Long Beach, California, n.d.**

uninterested in exploring these deeper connections visually they instead, for the most part, chose to depict trains in a vacuum. Without making reference to the material world beyond the tracks, or without including the railroad's physical plant in their frames, Beebe and his cohorts offer only a partial glimpse of what the mid-century railroad landscape looked like. For them, this was the stated goal. However, for a viewer such as myself, with an interest in "sense of place" and an eye toward social, economic, and architectural history, this type of photography falls a bit short. But the snapshot, which constitutes the output of a *third* type of railfan photography done during this same time frame—and distinct from the photos the roster and action shooters were making—fills in the gaps (see, for example, p. 142, above and right).

Snapshooters—with their diverse interests, (unintentional) inclusive style, and haphazard modes of "seeing"—played a heretofore little-recognized role in the artistic development of railroad photography in the first half of the twentieth century. These amateurs, unacquainted for the most part with the finer points of photographic composition, exposure, and lighting, were similarly unconcerned with making epic pictures of trains at speed. For them the simple snapshot,

unskilled, rough cut, and made on the run with inexpensive equipment, sufficed. As two-dimensional vignettes of recent history, these snapshots recorded both significant and mundane moments in the railroad world and the railfan's life: watching a hostler and workmen fill a locomotive's sand dome on an excursion run (p. 121), exploring the aftereffects of a tragic derailment, picturing a fellow coworker doing maintenance work on passenger cars, commemorating the last run with a photo of the engine crew or an unadorned snap of a freight car or coaling tower or some other seemingly insignificant aspect of railroad infrastructure deemed interesting (p. 80). Inclusive and unfiltered and occasionally emotional, these everyday views of railroading were taken for the best and most sincere reason: because one wants to.

After spending several years examining vernacular railroad photographs I now feel an alternative history for American railroad photography could be written. Previously I assumed significant print agencies of the era—*Life* magazine, Beebe's plethora of books, rotogravure Sunday paper supplements, or the rise of railfan photojournalism in the form of *Trains* and its influential editor David P. Morgan—were the primary shapers of a fresh vision for train photography in this country. Novel photographic ideas, based on images they published, flowed from these institutions and were absorbed, imitated, integrated, and embellished by talented amateurs. Even so, a from-the-bottom-up

Photographer unknown, Railroad unknown,
Man with bicycles and passenger train,
location unknown, n.d.

F. A. Cole, Chicago, Lehigh Valley Railroad,
Head-on collision between Camelbacks #1666 and #725,
Jersey City, New Jersey, February 26, 1916.

Photographer unknown, Railroad unknown, *Freight with steam locomotive comes toward camera*, location unknown, 1956.

action was occurring simultaneously, with the snapshot rising from the depths of its everyday ordinariness to a similar prominence of impact, defining anew how we see. Remember that thousands of images circulated within the International Engine Picture Club's fraternal ranks and became a de facto reference library (as did all types of the vernacular photography railfans collected and looked at). The snapshots' diversity in subject matter and point of view and the strange brew of aesthetics (off-kilter framing, bad exposures, jagged cropping, a photographer's shadow falling within the image, or blurred figures in the foreground) perhaps broadened pictorial possibilities for all railfans. These factors, which later became known as the "snapshot aesthetic," very probably influenced the artistic advance of railroad photography in America just as these same strategies—appropriated and refined in the 1950s, '60s, and '70s by the likes of Robert Frank, Lee Friedlander, and William Eggleston—prefigured new trends for fine-art photography to follow.

No photo historian in 2013 would deny every type of photographic practice has affected the evolution of the art form since its beginnings, including the snapshot. But this may not have been evident sixty-five years ago. Beaumont Newhall, in his seminal book *The History of Photography: 1839 to the Present*, published in 1937, made no reference whatsoever to amateur photography and its possible artistic influences on the medium,[26] which is why previous analyses of railroad photography have not necessarily considered this genre relevant.

The snapshot, therefore, according to the photo historian Geoffrey Batchen—which constitutes the majority of all photographs ever produced[27]—had made its humble presence known in a subtle but lasting way in the railfan world. I posit that through its plainspoken examination of everyday life we see a fulsome account of the railroad milieu in the first half of the twentieth century, a viewpoint that encompassed far more than the three-quarter-view school with its more narrow focus ever could. This expanded vision gave future photographers, historians, anthropologists, urban geographers, and photo collectors a wealth of information to analyze, appreciate, and be influenced by.

Nothing Other Than What They Are

OUTSIDE THE MARGINS OF THE TWO traditions of railfan photography described above, and setting the snapshot discussion aside, other pictures published in this book have an interesting variety in style, approach, and intended use. Professional and amateur-made images abound. Discolored, torn, tattered, and creased 8 x 10s, discarded by defunct railroad publicity or claims departments, form a segment of the collection. Pictures made for valuation purposes (an interesting historical turn for rail photography, discussed below) forms another. Postcards peddled by small-town itinerant photographers also make the cut. Glass plates, stereographs, and cabinet cards stake a claim for territory here as well. All of these types of photos, collectively referred to as vernacular, "found," or anonymous photographs, are reflections of the common everyday visual language of ordinary people[28] and, for our purposes, act as modest portals into the world of late-nineteenth- and early to mid-twentieth-century railroading, documenting its history, traditions, and social relations and the physical plants and landscapes railroads inhabit.

No one knows in every case precisely where the photos came from, why or for whom they were taken, nor the intended audience for their reception. But within the selection of images in this book we can make educated guesses (often aided by actual information on the back of the prints) about the role documentary photography has had in differing contexts over time. All the photos merit historical discussion and study, of course, but that's beyond the scope of the present project. Instead, I've selected a few categories for review and interpretation.

Evidentiary Photography

So far as possible, photographs should show the matter
depicted in the most neutral straight-forward manner.
The photographer should be cautioned against producing
dramatic effects; any drama in the photograph should emanate
from the subject matter alone, and not from affected photographic techniques or unusual camera angles. . . . Photographs
made this way would have a sense of accuracy about them and
an aura of objectivity.

—S. G. Erhlich[29]

Commercial or industrial photographers—in the
service of railroad claims departments that needed
visual documentation for accident reports or lawsuits—
made several of the images in this book. These
photographers were either in-house railroad employees,
cameramen retained by insurance carriers, or for-hire
journeymen who ran local studios and could be called
in at a moment's notice. Made for evidentiary use in
the courtroom, these photographs described in accurate,
irrefutable photographic terms aspects of a case being
litigated. Often they were scene-of-the-crime photos
taken months after the fact: a lonely grade crossing

adjacent to a country road that was the site of an auto
accident; shots detailing bad track or a faulty switch
frog that caused a derailment; an outsize locomotive
cylinder head that presented clearance problems as an
engine neared the roundhouse resulting in the injury
of a worker.

Liberated from their original use, these same
photographs strike us as mysterious; they accrue
new meaning and can be read in various ways. The
grade crossing photograph, once a site of accidental
tragedy, is now a bucolic landscape of quiet valley
and low-slung foothills, a view plucked from a

J.J. Griffin, Pennsylvania Railroad, *4-6-2 in yard scene with
automobile,* Atlantic City, New Jersey, August 1957.

Frederick J. Weber, Long Island Rail Road
Photo made for evidentiary purposes in grade crossing accident
Aquebogue, New York, September 2, 1936. (Queens Borough
Public Library Collection, Long Island Division)

period *Sunset* magazine spread (pp. 56–57). In the image (pp. 120–21) explaining a freight yard mishap—where suit-and-tie middle managers roam uncomfortably over a network of rails, pointing here and there ("this is where it happened; this is what we're talking about")—we witness a scene of surrealist absurdity, suggestive of photographs by the artist John Baldessari toying with bizarre juxtaposition and recontextualization. The truncated image (p. 87) of a steam locomotive near an engine house wall becomes an artistic arrangement of light and dark / positive and negative space bordering on abstraction—not quite Charles Sheeler's photograph *Wheels* from 1939 but nonetheless an image that displays the industrial brawn of the machine age and, though unintended, a good example of modernist photography.

In-house railroad company photos documenting the esoteric construction of a freight car being rebuilt in Terre Haute, Indiana (pp. 272–73), showing a newly installed interlocking panel at Los Angeles Union Passenger Terminal in 1939 (p. 203), or depicting the proper way to give hand signals when riding atop a boxcar (pp. 184–85) are the kinds of images that also fit into this evidentiary, matter-of-fact category. The railroads required photographs competently made, pictures that rendered information clearly whether they be used for publicity, historical documentation, or insurance, education, and safety purposes.

Other images, such as those by H. F. Brown, exist as proof of someone's pleasure in recording the engineering marvels of the man-made railroad landscape: tunnel portals, right-of-ways, bridges, abutments, overhead catenary, and pole towers (pp. 88–89 and 132). Scientific in tone, Brown's small 3 x 4 proof prints of the Hell Gate bridge construction from 1915–17, chronicling a rising sculpture spanning sky

and river, are reminiscent of the nineteenth-century descriptive photography of the French photographer Édouard Baldus.[30] A gifted amateur using state-of-the-art equipment, Brown marked the progress of the bridge's erection with these time-lapse images: did he go daily, once a week, or once a month? As a member of the engineering department on the New Haven Railroad from 1910 to 1952 he also incessantly photographed other facets of the electrified lines, as his other images in this volume attest, with access to many off-limits locations (see pp. 100 and 108).

More curious but similar to Brown's images are the generic photographs of various railroads' physical plants and landscapes (see pp. 190–91 and see 216–17), many produced perhaps for the Valuation Act of 1913. Congress mandated that every railroad must map and photographically document its assets, including "equipment, motive power, towers, bridges and more," in order for the Interstate Commerce Commission to determine fair freight rates. These photos, taken by survey teams, company photographers, or hired hands range in quality from well-crafted large-format studies to carelessly done snapshots taken with postcard cameras; apparently no strict guidelines dictated how the pictures got made.[31] Inventorying began in 1914 and wasn't completed until around 1928. This vast photographic archive was periodically updated by common carriers through the early 1960s (for valuation, insurance, and historical purposes) when a new structure was built or track improvements were made. The unintended consequence of this costly government directive, which chagrined the railroads but later proved a boon to historians and prototype modelers, was the creation of a substantive archive with architectural if not always cultural merit. Sadly, as railroads collapsed into bankruptcy or succumbed to mergers through the latter half of the twentieth century, much of this visual history was lost; corporate archives were dumped (paper records, photo albums, prints and negatives) with little regard for conserving the past. Some concerned technical societies or gung ho individuals arrived in time, but for most it was much too late. Photo collections, if saved at all, were scattered piecemeal.

Though it seems most railroads discarded wholesale their portion of such valuation material,

Photographer unknown, Delaware, Lackawanna & Western Railroad
Documentation of station architecture, main line, and grounds
Nicholson, Pennsylvania, n.d. (Jim Shaughnessy Collection)

Photographer unknown, Delaware, Lackawanna & Western Railroad
Documentation of station architecture, main line, and grounds
Clarks Summit, Pennsylvania, n.d. (Jim Shaughnessy Collection)

a partial, very incomplete set of this photographic survey still resides in the National Archives[32] as well as in a few public institutional collections, for example, the Cleveland Memory Project housed at the Michael Schwartz Library at Cleveland State University, which has a large repository of valuation photos depicting railroads such as the Wheeling and Lake Erie and the Newburgh and South Shore.[33] As essential documents of our former industrial heritage—and excellent references to what existed by the nation's right-of-ways in urban and rural areas—it remains an underexamined intersection between railroads and photography and deserving of further scholarship and research.

Stylistically, as Erhlich's quote above suggests, all these evidentiary-type pictures lack authorial presence and inherent drama; they don't pretend to be anything other than what they are. Surprisingly, however, this banality rings with honesty, gives them understated authority, and arouses our curiosity about their histories and meaning. While perhaps not beautiful in a traditional sense, these images nonetheless can reward aesthetic contemplation and expand the boundaries of what is worth looking at: a goal the best art accomplishes.

Views, Stereographs, and Cabinet Cards

LANDSCAPE PHOTOGRAPHERS OF THE LATE nineteenth and early twentieth centuries found the allure of twinned rails disappearing into the distance an irresistible subject for their ground glass. Lensmen such as William Rau, William Henry Jackson, L. C. McClure, Alfred A. Hart, Carleton Watkins, and others made it a repetitive motif (see pp. 210–11 and pp. 220–21).[34] Vanishing-point perspectives evoked mysterious stirrings of wanderlust, while simultaneously capturing the grandeur of the railroad's physicality situated in an expansive geography. Landforms, scale, and mass were the plastic elements these artists paid attention to when creating their "views" or "scenics." A favorite visual device used by cameramen to measure the vastness of the mountainous West or the valleyed East was to place a human figure centered in the frame. William Rau, traveling the Pennsylvania Railroad in a private car to photograph along its main lines, often used a flagman near the rear of the train for this purpose (pp. 228–29).[35] Such a pictorial tactic not only dramatized the grandness of the landscape traversed by the railroad, scalewise, but helped humanize an earthly space that might otherwise be

construed as foreboding by late-nineteenth-century psyches conditioned to regard nature as "wildering" and dangerous rather than as places of sublime tranquillity and beauty.[36]

The topographic studies by these photographers often had a detached emotional tone; nonetheless, the images registered feelings of veneration and reverence. Made for advertising or documentation purposes, and requiring great technical finesse, gargantuan cameras, and wagonloads of additional equipment, the photographs were effective in luring urbanites and rural folk alike to climb aboard passenger trains and "see the world." To our contemporary eye and global mind-set, where no corner of our planet remains photographically undiscovered, and our sense of awe is diminished, they now appear quaint and unremarkable. But to a person alive in 1898 these same images had a transportive effect. The stereograph, a popular entertainment in late-nineteenth-century America, "displayed views of far-away lands, making the travel experience, through photography, available to everyone"[37] (see pp. 76–77). Mammoth prints, 18 x 21 and larger, made from these practitioners'

large-format negatives, produced ready-to-hang photographs ("views") suitable for parlor display, a common form of home decoration in America's late Victorian era.[38]

Jackson, Watkins, Hart, and McClure also routinely had their landscape images converted to stereographs and cabinet cards (all mounted on heavy cardstock with descriptive typeset captions on the back), either under their own volition or by entrepreneurs who appropriated their work without payment or acknowledgment, a common practice for

Photographer unknown, Colorado Central Railroad
Passenger train on Georgetown Loop Trestle
Georgetown, Colorado, n.d.

William Henry Jackson, Denver & Rio Grande Railroad
"Engine 99 'Kokomo' and Engine 46 'Bandito' on passenger train in Veta Pass"
Colorado, c. 1890s.

the day.[39] These portable mementoes made their way into the general population throughout the country. One source of this diaspora was so-called butcher boys—young men selling sundry items aboard transcontinental trains in the late 1800s. Collected as souvenirs of remembrance, passengers bought them to help recall the majestic landscapes they'd passed through but couldn't experience firsthand. Jackson, perhaps the most commercially minded landscape photographer of the era, once received a contract for 10,000 cards.[40] A large print run/order for the time, it attests to the popularity of photographic views within the emerging mass-market economy of the mid- to late nineteenth century.

These populist forms of keepsakes ended up tucked away in albums, attics, or scrapbooks. Handed down through succeeding generations, they were either kept in the family or sold to interested third parties. Just as this photographica circulates today unceasingly through various distribution channels, railfans of the International Engine Picture Club era (and those fans involved in the hobby prior to its inception) also coveted similar collectibles, for either their historic value or their elegant beauty. Like their contemporary analog they, too, archived them, collected them, and sometimes cast them quickly back into the swift current of downstream trade.

A POPULAR SUBJECT FOR PHOTO postcards in the early twentieth century was trains. Depicting the railroad in all its glory (or infamy), they were produced for myriad reasons: as souvenirs commemorating a tragic derailment; as pieces of small-town boosterism highlighting a freight yard or station; or those honoring a record harvest filling an endless string of flatcars (see left and opposite). Portraits were common too. We see train or work crews classically arranged or positioned as if in a police lineup—all stiff-posed and dour-faced—not smiling for the camera (see pp. 144–45) because it was not fashionable to do so.

In an era prior to our contemporary worldwide media that report events as they occur (or tell us about not one but multiple daily disasters), a local train wreck in the early 1900s would have been an extraordinary occurrence and a significant historical moment (see pp. 174–75). Hometown and itinerant photographers, who derived part of their incomes from selling real-photo postcards of news events, would arrive on the scene to document the somber aftermath. In a time before newspaper halftones became common, these photographers acted as the public's eye and trusted witness. Printing postcards in small batches of one hundred or fewer for quick local consumption, these 3 x 5 pieces of paper became the physical evidence of *that which had taken place*, souvenirs certifying daily existence. These were readily available at the usual main street locations: drugstore, novelty shop, newsstand, the photographer's studio.

If not shot on a postcard-size negative, images were cropped to fit the horizontal format. The photographer etched a title onto the negative in backward lettering with India ink, sometimes adding a number to facilitate reordering. Or perhaps the lensman had a Kodak 122 folding camera with a sliding window in the back that allowed the photographer to inscribe the negative (without exposing it) right after taking the picture.

Considering the importance of the railroad theme for small-town photographers everywhere, it's not unreasonable to speculate that many of these homey prints also found there way into the collections of interested railfans. The postcard's "emphasis on inclusion, and directness and abundance of information"[41]

also matched the snapshot's defining attributes, which leads one to believe that postcards' knack for contextualization was a contributing influence in the evolution of railfan photography in America, even if on the subliminal level.

The Importance of Preservation

THE PICTURES I ACQUIRED at Springfield had most likely, at one point or another, come from a collection of a person newly deceased, or perhaps passed down from friend to friend, historical society to historical society, as treasured items given safe haven by temporary custodians. Even these acts of guardianship couldn't forestall their inevitable arrival into the marketplace for dispersal. On the one hand I experience a personal sadness in seeing the photographs cast adrift. For me, they represent their makers' commitment, with much toil and time invested. Selling them at swap meets, as inexpensive items quickly disposed of, seems an affront, an act of marginalization. But then again finding these castoffs, bringing them back from the brink of anonymity and cultural abandonment, feels to me like a rescue mission of the best kind. And

maybe that's the point: in being recycled this material may eventually find a proper home. In its temporary discarded state, in that interval between seller and new buyer, it again becomes interesting and valuable.

Tracking the history of a photographer's archive and how it made its way to the marketplace would be an interesting case study. From the numerous stories I've heard, it can be an epic and sometimes trying journey. Relatives left with massive archives to manage often don't know what they have, whom to contact, or how to go about disposing of such a vast quantity of material. In other instances a disenfranchised spouse, angry at her husband's time-consuming train buff activities—activities that often took precedent over family—relegates his negatives and slides to the nearest dumpster in a final act of retribution.

Photographer unknown, Great Northern Railway
Postcard of freight yard scene, Willmar, Minnesota, n.d.

Photographer unknown, Fort Smith & Western Railroad
Postcard of people and freight train with record hay shipment
Castle, Oklahoma, November 3, 1912.

Too often these collections are treated with little regard for their historic or aesthetic value and either get lost or, if somewhat luckier, become monetized and broken up to find their way into other people's archives through fellow collectors, antiques dealers, or vending entrepreneurs. When someone passes away, close friends are usually called in and get first dibs, cherry-picking the best material. In many cases that's fine, and the most representative work is saved for posterity. But the downside to this equation can't be ignored; the "best work" now resides in private hands and is not accessible to the public. Once the close peers of the photographer are gone, buyers specializing in railroadiana arrive. These folks, usually well known in the fraternity, maintain close connections to the railfan community and often aid families in deaccessioning a collection grown over a lifetime, which can be a herculean task. This is to the good. Now the secondary and tertiary photographs find new life: interesting imagery missed by the first responders gets picked up by other collectors and then the remaining material, which may not have much aesthetic value artistically, gets sold to modelers (as in the case at Springfield) as documents critical to their historical research. Unfortunately, this rush to cash in on a deceased family member's prized possessions, which often represents the lifework of a rail historian, a locomotive expert, or an aficionado of a particular railroad, deals a critical blow to future scholarship and utilization.

Fragmenting or scattering a collection "to the wind" partially negates its research value as social history, or as a record of one person's perspective and interpretation of any given period of American railroading. An archive such as this, housed at a variety of institutions in various cities, is analogous to having to travel to different libraries in order to read consecutive chapters of a novel no longer under one cover. Not what one wants to do when seeking information and performing essential research.

The corporate photo archives that railroads generated for their own internal uses—images made for publicity, for safety training purposes, or for publication in in-house magazines and bulletins—sometimes suffered a fate similar to the valuation images and the private collections mentioned above. Some archives were rescued, some stolen, some passed off to historical societies, some stashed in attics and basements awaiting proper care and storage. Others are still in holding patterns looking for a home. It appears a few major railroads' picture archives did survive (the Union Pacific and the Norfolk Southern, née Norfolk and Western, come to mind), but many were not as fortunate; a large percentage of railroading's documented visual culture was tossed and lost. Sadly, more than one story has been told of hearing the thunderous crash of glass-plate negatives as a railroad's pictorial record landed in the trash can.

THE ARCHIVE AND PRESERVATION QUESTION—how the photographs should be organized, how to care for them, and where they should go—looms large today in the railfan world. The eldest members of our fraternity, photographers alive during the steam-to-diesel transition, are passing away and leaving vast collections behind, sometimes in a state of disarray, sometimes meticulously arranged. Although institutions can't or won't acquire every collection offered them they are, for the most part, eager to accept historical material relevant to their mission, which can be either nationally or regionally focused. (Yale's Beinecke Library specializes in western Americana; the University of Connecticut at Storrs' main interest lies in northeastern railroads with an emphasis on the New Haven Railroad.) But even this scenario can be problematic. Many institutions in these fiscally challenging times grapple with budgetary constraints even when they do acquire a collection, often not having the means to process it. But as photographers (and perhaps future donors), this is where we need to step in: our work doesn't end with the taking of photographs. More is required if we're concerned about the legacy of our collections living on and being utilized to their fullest potential as resource material.

To this end it's important that our archives are in a form that can be easily transferred to a university or historical society setting. Public institutions and organizations, for example, the Center for Railroad Photography and Art (with archives at Lake Forest College in Illinois), while open to all possible acquisition scenarios, are more inclined to welcome a collection if it is contacted, scanned, archivally secure (negatives, prints, and ephemera properly sleeved in inert materials), chronologically or geographically organized, and annotated with accurate information. In this state, coupled with a substantial financial gift or endowment, such a collection would be readily welcomed, the envy of every institutional archivist. Thus assembled it also becomes a valuable tool for railroad historians or cultural anthropologists who want to know what past train photographers saw and how life looked *then*.

Tributaries of Talent:
In Praise of Vernacular Railroad Photographs

THE BEST PART OF COLLECTING vernacular railroad images these past ten years is that the experience itself, beyond the thrill of the purchase, launched me into ever widening fields of inquiry. I delved into historical research, examining bodies of work previously unknown to me. I read further into the popular literature of the time. As I stitched together the story of railfanning's cultural development as a broad-based fraternal system, I more fully understood the influence those networks had in helping produce the rich trove of railroad imagery we enjoy today. This, in turn, led me down other tangential paths.

Further research broadened my appreciation of nineteenth-century and early-twentieth-century photography. I was compelled, for instance, to think about creative progressions. How did earlier photography of railroad subjects, especially the work done by non-railfan journeymen photographers, inform the train photos made by following generations? And as newer pictorial styles emerged did they carry the time-honored traditions forward in a marginal way or trigger a bolder advance for the art form?

Studying snapshots for this project instilled in me a deeper understanding of the aesthetic value of the nonmasterpiece, which requires a suspension of typical notions about what constitutes art, and an ability to embrace the mundane or banal as aesthetic categories in and of themselves. Taken by amateurs, these photos possess a naive grace. As adjunct tributaries of a broad talent pool flowing into one great stream of railfan imagery, photographers who made these types of pictures were so numerous and diverse in number that their influence on the field is difficult to reconstruct or assess. Yet they certainly need to be considered.

By including the works of railroad photography's *other*—the anonymous or underrepresented picture takers—we are afforded the opportunity to expand the conversation about its aesthetic and historical development. And we are also given a chance to honor and remember additional members of the unsung: the commercial and industrial photographers employed by studios hired by railroads and the ordinary people with Brownie box cameras, whose photos never graced the pages of *Trains, Railroad,* or other fan magazines.

The whole adventure reinforced for me what every researcher knows, that the inquiry is never finished; all histories are polysemous; there is never just a single version or vantage point from which to learn. Such is the case in studying the account of train photography's advance as an art form in the United States of America.

JOHN SZARKOWSKI ONCE SAID about photographs that "the image would survive the subject, and become the remembered reality."[42] This potent aphorism succinctly reminds us why collecting vernacular photographs is so satisfying. We behold a picture containing content that no longer exists, created by a photographer no longer alive. And yet the picture's latent reality miraculously rises from its surface, existing for us in the present as an accurate likeness of the past. Holding a snapshot or glossy 8 x 10 railroad photograph in my hands, then, and contemplating the circumstances surrounding its production, producer, and place in time is still a magical experience, even after a decade of avid collecting.

Photographer unknown, New York Central Railroad
Freight train with 2-8-2 #1506 on secondary main line
Ohio, n.d.

Photographs

1
———

(previous spread)
Wally Johnson
East Carolina Railway
4-6-0 #1031 making time
near a country road
Tarboro, North Carolina
mid-1950s.

2
———

H. Reid
Norfolk & Portsmouth
Belt Line Railroad
Father and son
admire 2-8-0 #16
Little Creek, Virginia
1954.

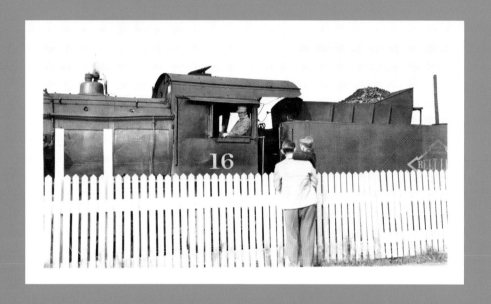

3
—

George Sanderson
New York Central Railroad
*Portrait of engineer in
cab of 4-6-0 #1015*
August 5, 1947.

4
—

Photographer unknown
Pennsylvania Railroad
Freight train with 2-8-0 #8527
Madisonville, Ohio
February 8, 1925.

5

C. T. Stoner,
Ann Arbor Railroad
Wreck on Huron River bridge
Ann Arbor, Michigan
January 17, 1904.

6

Frank Lisowelk
Essex Terminal Railway
*Ferris Wheel and freight
train with 0-6-0 #10*
Windsor, Ontario
April 1943.

7

—

Photographer unknown
Pennsylvania Railroad
*Worker walks by Baldwin
Centipede locomotive #5933*
Location unknown
n.d.

8

—

H. Reid
Baltimore & Ohio Railroad
Hostler washes 2-8-2 #372
Fairmont, West Virginia
August 1957.

9
—

Photographer unknown
Boston & Maine Railroad
Freight train with 2-8-4
#4013 waiting to haul freight
over Fitchburg Division
East Somerville, Massachusetts
May 1939.

10
—

F. Rodney Dirkes
Boston & Maine Railroad
4-6-2 #4102 steams up
near engine terminal
Boston, Massachusetts
July 23, 1927.

19. PHOTO. BY C.MCCLURE. DENVER.

11

L. C. McClure
Denver & Rio Grande Railroad
Freight train in Eagle River Canyon with
second track construction under way
Colorado, c. 1905.
(Richard A. Ronzio Collection)

12

H. Reid
Saint Elizabeth's Hospital Railroad
Photographer Ed Patterson, using
view camera under focusing cloth,
makes portrait of 0-4-0T #4
Washington, D. C.
early 1960s.

13

Photographer unknown
Railroad unknown
Photograph made from
rear of a passenger train
Location unknown
n.d.

14

Photographer unknown
Atchison, Topeka
& Santa Fe Railway
Track laborer
Coleman, Texas
January 19, 1909.

15

Photographer unknown
New York Central Railroad
4-8-2 on main line in silhouette
Location unknown
n.d.

16

———

Photographer unknown
Railroad unknown
Portrait of steam locomotive
Location unknown
n.d.

17

———

Photographer unknown
Denver & Rio Grande Railroad
*Passenger train in urban
setting with 4-6-0 #761*
Denver, Colorado
March 23, 1909.

18
—

Photographer unknown
Railroad unknown
Locomotive portrait of 4-4-0
Location unknown
n.d.

19
—

Photographer unknown
Railroad unknown
Possible motor vehicle /
pedestrian accident site
at railroad crossing
Location unknown
n.d.

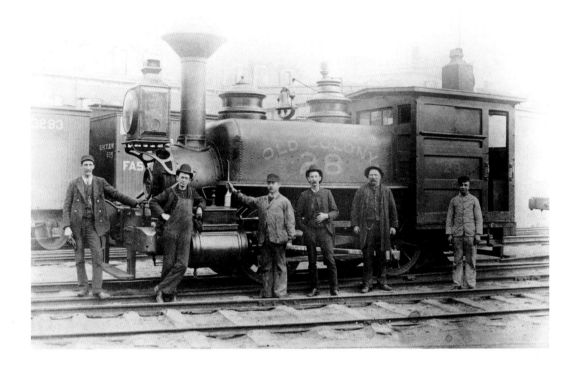

20

—

Photographer unknown
Old Colony Railroad
Portrait of 0-4-0T #28
"Monitor" with crew
Location unknown
c. 1870–80s.

21

—

H. Reid
Railroad unknown
Yard limit sign and
handcar section house
Location unknown
n.d.

22

—

E. D. Lindsley,
Herbert F. Smith Co.
Commercial Photographers
Delaware, Lackawanna
& Western Railroad
Evidentiary photograph
recording the scene of
automobile accident
Cortland, New York
November 5, 1920.

23

—

H. W. Pontin
Virginian Railway
*Portrait of Virginian
gondola #20031*
Location unknown
n.d.

24

—

Photographer unknown
Railroad unknown
Portrait of tank car
Location unknown
n.d.

25

H. Reid
Norfolk & Western Railroad
0-8-0 with water tank
Norfolk, Virginia
January 1957.

26

Philip R. Hastings
Chicago, Milwaukee
St. Paul & Pacific Railroad
*Freight train on High Bridge
trestle with 4-6-2 #889*
Marengo, Washington
1950s.

27

———

Photographer unknown
Rutland Railroad
Derailment in rural setting
with engines #869, #2039
and #2401, recto view
Rutland, Vermont
September 11, 1912.
(Jim Shaughnessy Collection)

28

—

Photographer unknown
Rutland Railroad
*Derailment in rural setting
with engines #869, #2039
and #2401, verso view*
Rutland, Vermont
September 11, 1912.
(Jim Shaughnessy Collection)

29

——

Photographer unknown
Pennsylvania Railroad
Freight train with 2-10-0 #4240
East of Altoona, Pennsylvania
n.d.

30

——

Photographer unknown
Rutland Railroad
Engine terminal scene
Rutland, Vermont
n.d.

31

___

Rail Photo Service
Great Northen Railway
Passenger train highballing through
countryside with 4-8-2 #2510
near Whitefish, Montana
n.d.

FARMERS GRAIN & SHIPPING CO. TRAIN. No.1.

AT STARKWEATHER. N.D. WINTER OF 1916. ENG. No 3.

32

Ora Deal
Great Northern Railway
"Farmers Grain & Shipping Co.
Train No. 1" with 2-6-0 #3
Starkweather, North Dakota
1916.

33

Photographer unknown
Long Island Rail Road
"Herman at 88th Street Crossing"
Location unknown
1948.

34

Photographer unknown
Baltimore & Ohio Railroad
Logo on B & O bus on ferry
Jersey City, New Jersey
June 13, 1937.

35

Carl Stillwell
Baltimore & Ohio Railroad
Yard scene with coaling tower
Grafton, West Virginia
August 2, 1966.

36

H. Reid
East Tennessee & Western
North Carolina Railroad
*Looking out of roundhouse
door at 2-8-0 #280*
Johnson City, Tennessee
late 1950s.

37

———

Ted G. Wurm
Nevada Consolidated Copper /
Nevada Northern Railway
Locomotive portrait of 0-6-2T #72
Ruth, Nevada, July 12, 1939.

38

———

Ted G. Wurm
Nevada Consolidated Copper /
Nevada Northern Railway
Locomotive portrait of 0-6-2T #501
Ruth, Nevada, July 12, 1939.

Keystone View Company's
Manufacturers and Publishers.

39

B. L. Lingley
Colorado Central Railroad
Stereograph of train on Georgetown Loop
Georgetown, Colorado, 1898.

2367—The "Loop," Georgetown, Col., U. S. A.

40

———

Photographer unknown
Pennsylvania Railroad
Freight train heading east
on Rockville Bridge
Rockville, Pennsylvania
n.d.

41

———

Photographer unknown
Long Island Rail Road
4-6-0 #31 at speed with
the Greenport Express
Bethpage Junction, New York
March 26, 1941.

42

Photographer unknown
Railroad unknown
Coaling tower and engine facility
Location unknown
n.d.

43

Photographer unknown
New York, New Haven
& Hartford Railroad
*Railroad enthusiasts' fantrip
detraining in Maybrook Yard*
Maybrook, New York
1955.

44

Philip R. Hastings
Rutland Railroad
Passenger train departs station
Location unknown, 1950s.
(Jim Shaughnessy Collection)

45

Ted G. Wurm
Virginia & Truckee Railroad
*4-6-0s #27 and #26 snowbound
digging out in Washoe Valley*
near Reno, Nevada
January 1937.

46

———

H. F. Brown
New York, New Haven
& Hartford Railroad
*4-6-2 #1388 coming
off of the electrified line
near Cedar Hill Yard*
New Haven, Connecticut
n.d.

47

———

C. Salley Jr.
New York Elevated Railroad
Tracks and railroad bridges
Brooklyn, New York
n.d.

48

———

Photographer unknown
Delaware, Lackawanna
& Western Railroad
*Photograph made for a personal
injury insurance claim, showing
scant clearance between 4-6-2
and roundhouse wall*
Scranton, Pennsylvania
November 5, 1924.

49
—

H. F. Brown
New York, New Haven
& Hartford Railroad
Standard signal anchor
bridge and main lines
Location unknown
1914.

B1295

50

Photographer unknown
Reading Railroad
4-6-2 #110 at engine
terminal with automobiles
Location unknown
October 1951.

51

Photographer unknown
Atlantic City & Shore Railroad
Streetcar #109 in boardwalk setting
Atlantic City, New Jersey
1940s?

52

—

Philip R. Hastings
Rutland Railroad
4-8-2 #91 acts as helper
in middle of freight train
Location unknown, 1950.
(Jim Shaughnessy Collection)

53

—

H. Reid
Virginia & Carolina
Southern Railway
Freight train approaches
country store with signs
Dublin, North Carolina
late 1950s.

54

—

Photographer unknown
Florida East Coast Railway
Passenger train going over
concrete-arched viaduct
Long Key, Florida
before 1935.

55

——

H. Reid
Norfolk & Western Railway
Two 4-8-0 helpers running light
Shawsville, Virginia
1950s.

56

———

Alexander Smith Co.
Pennsylvania Railroad
28th Street Yard ready
engine storage tracks
Pittsburgh, Ohio
1951

57

———

Photographer unknown
Pennsylvania Railroad
Portrait of trainman in
hat and leather jacket
holding handrail
of 4-8-2 #6719
Location unknown
n.d.

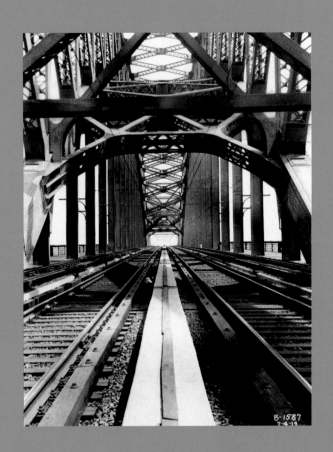

58

H. F. Brown
New York, New Haven
& Hartford Railroad
*View from on the
Hell Gate Bridge*
New York, New York
July 7, 1919.

59

Photographer unknown
Boston & Albany Railroad
*Steam locomotive with
crane on railroad bridge*
Springfield, Massachusetts
n.d.

H. Reid
East Tennessee & Western
North Carolina Railroad
*Portrait of 2-8-0 locomotive
and conductor Cy Crumley*
Johnson City, Tennessee
late 1950s.

61

―

John Pickett
Norfolk & Western Railway
4-8-2 locomotive in roundhouse
Norfolk, Virginia
April 1956.

62
—

(previous spread)
Photographer unknown
New York, Ontario & Western Railway
Passenger train on Ferndale trestle
Ferndale, New York
April 22, 1943.

63
—

Photographer unknown
New York, Ontario & Western Railway
4-4-0 being scrapped near roundhouse
Location unknown
n.d.

64
—

W. A. Ranke
Chicago & North Western Railway
Scrapping scene dismantling locomotives
Chicago, Illinois
February 3, 1940.

1479

B1479

65

H. F. Brown
New York, New Haven
& Hartford Railroad
*Hell Gate Bridge construction
and view of approach*
New York, New York
1915–16.

66

H. F. Brown
New York, New Haven
& Hartford Railroad
Hell Gate Bridge construction
New York, New York
1915–16.

67
—

W. R. McGee
Northern Pacific Railway
4-6-2 #2239 with mail
train in snowy landscape
Location unknown
n.d.

68
—

Photographer unknown
Northern Central Railroad
Train in pastoral scene
Marysville, Pennsylvania
c. 1890s.

69
—

H. F. Brown
Pennsylvania Railroad
Broad Street Station
Philadelphia, Pennsylvania
before June 1923.

70
—

Photographer unknown
Erie Railroad
Two Camelback locomotives
on Starrucca Viaduct
Lanesboro, Pennsylvania
late 1800s.

71

Photographer unknown
New York Central Railroad
4-6-2 #4914 with passenger train
Chicago, Illinois
n.d.

72

—

Photographer unknown
Rutland Railroad
Yard scene with roundhouse
Rutland, Vermont, c. 1895.
(Jim Shaughnessy Collection)

73

———

Photographer unknown
Delaware, Lackawanna
& Western Railroad
Yard scene with railfans
returning from an excursion
Bangor, Pennsylvania
October 22, 1939.

74

———

Ed Nowak
New York Central
Harmon shops turntable
and locomotive
Harmon, New York
June 11, 1945.
(Victor Hand Collection)

75

Photographer unknown
Norfolk & Western Railway
Baggage handler unloads
Railway Post Office car
Location unknown
n.d.

76

H. Reid
Norfolk & Portsmouth
Belt Line Railroad
Engine terminal scene
Port Norfolk, Virginia
1950s.

77

Photographer unknown
Pennsylvania Railroad
Inspecting switch point frog
as part of an accident report
Location unknown
June 16, 1948.

78

Photographer unknown
Reading Railroad
Hostler filling sand dome
during excursion trip
Location unknown
n.d.

79
—
Photographer unknown
Erie Railroad
Man in straw hat standing
trackside; 2-10-0 #4216
pusher on rear of train
Location unknown
n.d.

80
—
Photographer unknown
Chicago & North Western
and a consortium of 35
American Railroads
"Pioneer" locomotive,
performers and spectator,
Chicago Railroad Fair
Chicago, Illinois
1948–49.

81
—
(following spread)
Photographer unknown
Pennsylvania Railroad
Portrait of outside-braced
wood gondola #362548
Location unknown
n.d.

82

——

Photographer unknown
Rome, Watertown
& Ogdensburg Railroad
Portrait of railroad bridge
Location unknown
n.d.

83

——

Photographer unknown
Delaware & Hudson Railroad
View of hump in freight yard
Oneonta, New York
1920s.

84

Bob Bishop?
Denver & Salt Lake Railway
*Portrait of rotary snowplow
and railroaders*
Corona, Colorado
1926.

85

H. Reid
Fort Eustis, Army
Transportation Corps Railroad
Spare drivers and locomotives in snow
Newport News, Virginia
1950s.

Erie Canal
594C

86

Photographer unknown
New York Central Railroad
*Railroad tracks passing
under Erie Canal*
Rochester, New York?
n.d.

87

Katsusaburo Nishio
Japan National Railways
*View of 2-6-4T through
window of roundhouse
warming shed*
Ogaki, Japan, 1949.
(Ed Delvers Collection)

88

H. F. Brown
New York, Westchester
& Boston Railroad
Bridges over main lines
Woodlawn-Stamford,
Connecticut
n.d.

89

Philip R. Hastings
Rutland Railroad
*4-6-0 #71 departs station
with passenger train*
Rouses Point Junction,
New York, 1950s.
(Jim Shaughnessy Collection)

90

C. William Witbeck
Illinois Central Railroad
*Local freight train piloted by
two 0-6-0s and one 2-8-2
taken from window of
King Edwards Hotel*
Jackson, Mississippi
March 1941.
(David Price Collection)

91

Photographer unknown
Pennsylvania Railroad
Bridge and railroad tracks
Chicago, Illinois
n.d.

92
—

Donald W. Furler
Erie Railroad
4-6-2 #2935 with
the Erie Limited
Glen Rock, New Jersey
June 6, 1943

93

—

H. Reid
Norfolk & Portsmouth
Belt Line Railroad
*Locomotives and coaling
tower at engine terminal*
Port Norfolk, Virginia
1950s.

94

—

Photographer unknown
New York, New Haven
& Hartford Railroad
PA #0762 on train 179
Providence, Rhode Island
February 1961.

95

H. Reid
Railroad unknown
*Two men at depot
with passenger train*
Location unknown
n.d.

96

C. William Witbeck
Illinois Central Railroad
*Portrait of 0-8-0
#3563 and crew*
Mississippi
May 6, 1936.

97

———

Photographer unknown
Colorado & Southern Railway
4-6-0 #317 and warehouse buildings
Denver, Colorado
March 23, 1909.

98

———

H. Reid
Durham & Southern Railway
2-10-0 #202 and freight yard scene
Apex, North Carolina
1953.

99

Photographer unknown
New York Elevated Railroad
Portrait of locomotive and crew
Location unknown
n.d.

100

———

Photographer unknown
New York, Ontario & Western Railway
Portrait of 2-6-0 #138 and crew
Location unknown
c. 1900.

9820

101

Photographer unknown
Delaware & Hudson Railroad
*Portrait of 4-6-2 locomotive
boiler and firebox in mid-
assembly, negative #9820*
Colonie, New York, 1920?
(Jim Shaughnessy Collection)

102

Photographer unknown
Delaware & Hudson Railroad
Portrait of 4-6-2 locomotive
in mid-assembly, with boiler
jacketing on, frame and
firebox in place, negative #9821
Colonie, New York, 1920?
(Jim Shaughnessy Collection)

103

—

Photographer unknown
Railroad unknown
Covered railroad bridge as
seen from rear of caboose
Vermont?
n.d.

104

—

Leo R. Clark
Illinois Central Railroad
2-8-2 #1531 crosses
Illinois River bridge
Peoria, Illinois
n.d.

R.I WRECK 9/28/30 JENNINGS KAN

105

Photographer unknown
Illinois Central Railroad
Two views of a derailment
Location unknown
n.d.

106

Photographer unknown
Chicago, Rock Island
& Pacific Railroad
Train wreck and spectators
Jennings, Kansas
September 28, 1930.

107

Photographer unknown
Colorado & Southern Railway
Mixed freight train piloted
by 2-10-2 #902
Colorado, early 1950s.

108

Philip R. Hastings
Rutland Railroad
*Passenger train in
snow with 4-6-0 #78*
Cantic, Quebec, Canada,
1950s. (Jim Shaughnessy
Collection)

109

Frank Lisowelk
Essex Terminal Railway
2-6-0 #7 with freight train
Windsor, Ontario
July 1943.

110
—

Photographer unknown
Railroad unknown
Flooded tracks near
grain elevator
Location unknown
n.d.

111
—

Photographer unknown
Virginian Railway
Train #3 with 4-6-2 #210
and train #13 with 4-6-0 #201
during station stop
Mullens, West Virginia
late 1930s, early 1940s.

112

—

Rail Photo Service
Central Vermont Railway
Westbound freight train with
2-8-2 #3432 in winter scene
White River Junction, Vermont
1950s.

113

Photographer unknown
Baltimore & Ohio Railroad
Logo on crane
Grafton, West Virginia
August 28, 1964.

114

Photographer unknown
Pennsylvania Railroad
Detail of logo and
pin stripping on tender
Location unknown
n.d.

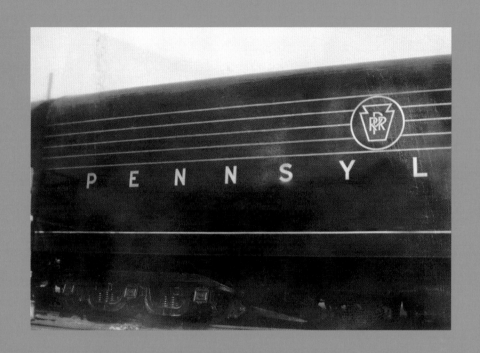

115

Phil H. Bonnet
Boston & Maine Railroad
Portrait of engineer in cab
Location unknown
June 5, 1937.

116

Photographer unknown
Baltimore & Ohio
Chicago Terminal Railroad
Engineman checks 2-6-0
#901 outside roundhouse
Chicago, Illinois
January 20, 1922.

117

Photographer unknown
Railroad unknown
*Portrait of damaged tank car
and workmen loading cart*
Location unknown
1920s–30s?

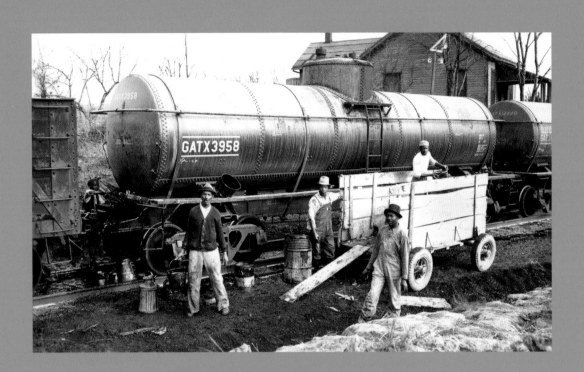

118

Photographer unknown
Railroad unknown
*Portrait of railroad workers
positioned around hand car*
Location unknown, c. 1880s?

119

C. William Witbeck
Illinois Central Railroad
Crew poses with 2-8-2 #1812
Mississippi, 1936.

120

H. F. Brown
New York, New Haven
& Hartford Railroad
Four men building catenary
Bridgeport, Connecticut
1914.

121

Photographer unknown
Railroad unknown
*Train track and lineman
climbing telephone pole*
Location unknown
n.d.

122
—

Photographer unknown
Pennsylvania Railroad
Portrait of Coal Wharf
East Altoona, Pennsylvania
November 4, 1943.

123

Jesse Wolley
Rutland Railroad
Two bicyclists converse;
4-4-0 with passenger train
and depot in background
Fort Ticonderoga, New York, 1920s.
(Jim Shaughnessy Collection)

124

(following spread)
Henry Huss
Pennsylvania Railroad
Train wreck aftermath
Location unknown, n.d.
(Taylor/Kelly Collection)

125

—

Jim Shaughnessy
Canadian National Railway
*Westbound passenger train
departs station with 4-8-4*
Burlington, Ontario
1956.

126

—

H. Reid
Railroad unknown
Looking out from rear of caboose
Location unknown
n.d.

127

—

Photographer unknown
Bangor & Aroostock Railroad
Locomotive and train crossing bridge
Location unknown
April 22, 1909.

128

—

John Pickett
Chicago, Burlington & Quincy Railroad
4-8-4 on wheat harvest extra at dusk
East of Galesburg, Illinois
November 1956.

129

—

Photographer unknown
Railroad unknown
*Passenger train in winter
landscape with 4-4-0*
Ohio, 1914.

Photographer unknown
Railroad unknown
Mainline tracks at dusk
Location unknown
n.d.

131

Photographer unknown
Southern Pacific Railroad
Men on top of boxcar
learning hand signals
Los Angeles, California, 1940s.
(Jeff Koeller Collection)

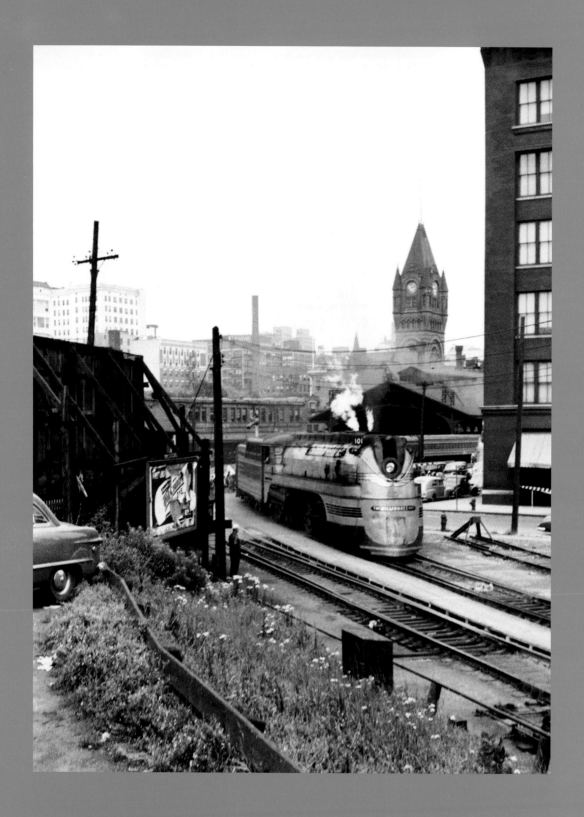

132

—

Photographer unknown
Chicago, Milwaukee
St. Paul & Pacific Railroad
Train 101 leaves downtown depot
Milwaukee, Wisconsin
n.d.

133

—

Photographer unknown
Pennsylvania Railroad
Portrait of streamlined
Pacific 4-6-2 #3768
Chicago, Illinois
April 26, 1936.

134
—

Photographer unknown
New York, New Haven
& Hartford Railroad
*Passenger train makes
a brief station stop*
Location unknown
n.d.

135
—

Charles A. Brown
Boston & Maine Railroad
Bicyclist admires 4-6-2 #3715
and passenger train at North Station
Boston, Massachusetts
April 1938.

136

Photographer unknown
Central New England Railway
Rural depot and yard scene
Silvernails, New York, c. 1921.
(Bob's Photos)

137
——

H. Reid
Chesapeake & Ohio Railroad
Fireless 0-6-0T #37 at rest in Elk Yard
South Charleston, West Virginia
1950s.

138
——

H. Reid
Norfolk & Western Railway
Fireman filling tender
Crewe, Virginia
late 1950s.

139

—

C. William Witbeck
Illinois Central Railroad
2-8-2 #1464 with freight
train enters yard as seen
from atop coaling tower
North Jackson, Mississippi
April 1938. (David Price
Collection)

140
—

H. L. Lambert
Pennsylvania Railroad
Freight train LR-508 on High Line
viaduct with yards in foreground
West Philadelphia, Pennsylvania
March 10, 1944.

141

Hanna and Hanna Studios
Atchison, Topeka & Santa Fe Railway
Locomotives and overhead
transfer crane in shop
Albuquerque, New Mexico
1913.

142

Photographer unknown
Great Northern Railway
Passenger train departing station
Minneapolis, Minnesota
n.d.

143

John Pickett
Boston & Maine Railroad
4-6-2 #3713 with
passenger train at speed
Ward Hill, Massachusetts
April 1946.

144
———
Photographer unknown
New York, New Haven
& Hartford Railroad
*Portrait of operator
at Neponset Bridge*
Quincy, Massachusetts
1947.

145
———
Photographer unknown
Southern Pacific Railroad
*View of interlocking plant
at LAUPT's Terminal Tower*
Los Angeles, California
1939.

146

(previous spread)
Fred Thatcher
Delaware & Hudson Railroad
*View of afternoon train with
the steamboat* Horicon *at right*
Lake George, New York, c. 1912.
(Jim Shaughnessy Collection)

147

William M. Rittase
Pennsylvania Railroad
*Philadelphia freight terminal
along Delaware River*
Philadelphia, Pennsylvania
1930–40s.

148

Photographer unknown
Hocking Valley Railroad
*Gondolas filled with sand
and coal in freight yard*
Presque Isle, Ohio, 1930.

149

Philip R. Hastings
Rutland Railroad
Engine terminal and freight yard
Rutland, Vermont, 1950s.
(Jim Shaughnessy Collection)

150

—

Photographer unknown
Railroad unknown
Excursionists on a break
Location unknown, n.d.

151

—

Photographer unknown
Denver & Rio Grande Railroad
*"View of western entrance
to the Royal Gorge"*
Royal Gorge, Colorado,
1899.

213

Photographer unknown
Ferrocarril Del Pacifico
*Maintenance worker cleaning
ex-Milwaukee Road
Hiawatha passenger car*
Location unknown
1950s?

153

Walter B. Redman
Empire & Southeastern Railway
Portrait of 4-4-0 #3 and crew
Empire Junction, Michigan
1915.

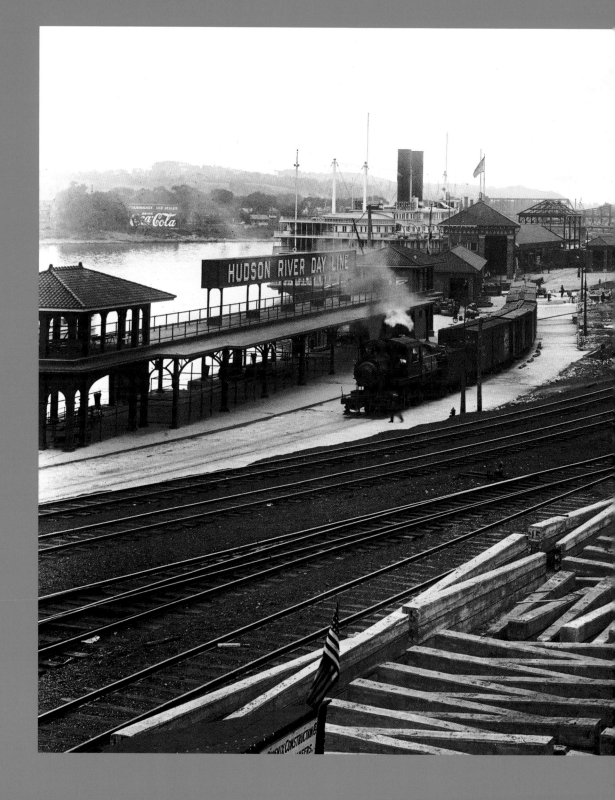

154
—

(previous spread)
Photographer unknown
Delaware & Hudson Railroad
*Photograph documenting office
building extension construction*
Albany, New York, June 16, 1923.
(Jim Shaughnessy Collection)

155
—

Photographer unknown
Public Service of New Jersey Railway
Streetcar #3206 at station stop
Newark, New Jersey, n.d.

156

Photographer unknown
Union Pacific Railroad
Stereograph of railroad bridge
Weber Canyon, Utah, n.d.

R. Bridge, Weber Canyon, Pacific Railro:

·SERIES·

AMERICAN

157

—

H. Reid
Railroad unknown
Trainmen re-railing
steam locomotive
Location unknown
September 30, 1947.

158

—

H. W. Pontin
New York, New Haven
& Hartford Railroad
4-6-2 #1355 at speed
with passenger train
Location unknown
n.d.

159

Photographer unknown
Hocking Valley Railroad
*J. T. Adams construction
train in freight yard*
Presque Isle, Ohio, 1930.

160

———

(previous spread)
Photographer unknown
Rutland Railroad
4-6-0 #20 with northbound
passenger train crosses East Creek
Rutland, Vermont, c. 1920.

161

———

William Rau?
Railroad unknown
Man and train tracks in landscape
Location unknown
September 14, 1917.

162

H. W. Pontin?
Boston & Maine Railroad
4-6-2s #3671 and #3652
as seen from water tower
at Somerville Yard
Boston, Massachusetts,
n.d.

163

Photographer unknown
Texas & Pacific Railway
2-8-2 #803 and coaling tower
Location unknown
n.d.

164

David Joslyn?
Southern Pacific Railroad
Rotary snowplow train
clearing Donner Pass
near Soda Springs, California
late 1940s–early 1950s.

Photographer unknown
Northern Pacific Railway
2-6-0 #453 with passenger
train at station stop
Vancouver, Washington
April 4, 1908.

166

Photographer unknown
Baltimore & Ohio Railroad
Engine terminal at night
with 2-8-2 #4591
Location unknown, n.d.

167

Don Ball Jr.
Reading Railroad
*4-8-4 in yard with
switch stand in foreground*
Location unknown
n.d.

168

Don Ball Jr.
Union Pacific Railroad
*4-12-2 #9084 with freight
train passes depot*
Lawrence, Kansas
November 25, 1950.

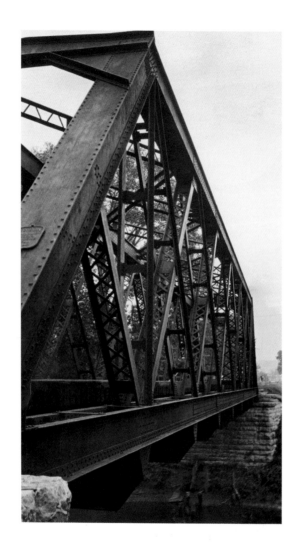

169

—

Photographer unknown
Rome, Watertown
& Ogdensburg Railroad
Detail of railroad bridge
Location unknown
n.d.

170

—

Photographer unknown
Rome, Watertown
& Ogdensburg Railroad
Detail of railroad bridge
Location unknown
n.d.

171

Photographer unknown
Chicago, Milwaukee
St Paul & Pacific Railroad
4-4-2 #1 at speed with
Hiawatha passenger train
Chicago, Illinois
October 1, 1946.

Southern Pacific (9)   JUN 1954   Owenyo, Cal.

172
—

Photographer unknown
Southern Pacific Railroad
Narrow-gauge 4-6-0 #9 switches
yard four months before retirement
Owenyo, California
June 1954.

173

Philip R. Hastings
Rutland Railroad
4-6-0 #51 and 2-8-0
#18 in engine terminal
Rutland, Vermont, 1950s.
(Jim Shaughnessy Collection)

174

———

H. Reid
Norfolk Southern Railway
2-8-0 on head end of special troop
train movement with Pullman cars
Norfolk, Virginia, environs, 1950s.

175

—

Photographer unknown
Railroad unknown
*View of freight yard used
for insurance claim purposes*
Location unknown
June 16, 1948

176

Philip R. Hastings
Rutland Railroad
Portrait of 4-6-0 #53 on turntable
Rouses Point, Vermont, 1940s.
(Jim Shaughnessy Collection)

177
—
J. K. Patch
Boston & Maine Railroad
Wreck of train #85
Near Deerfield, Massachusetts
April 7, 1886.

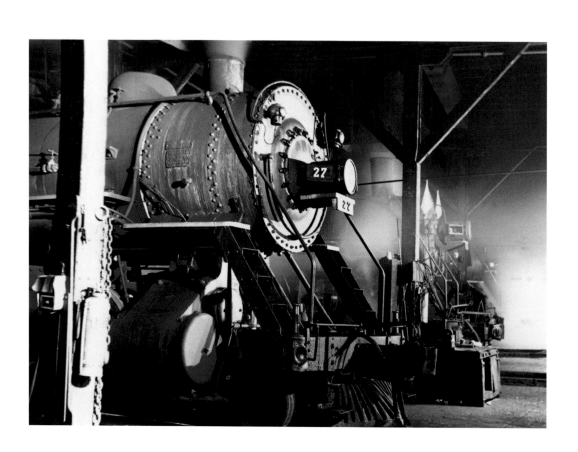

178

—

Philip R. Hastings
Rutland Railroad
Locomotives in roundhouse
Alburgh, Vermont, 1940s.
(Jim Shaughnessy Collection)

179

—

Philip R. Hastings
Rutland Railroad
0-6-0 #100 switches sleeper car
onto southbound "Mt Royal"
Burlington, Vermont, 1940s.
(Jim Shaughnessy Collection)

180–182
—

Photographer unknown
Delaware & Hudson Railroad
*Three portraits of 4-6-2 locomotive
assembly, negatives #9953,
#9957, and #10138*
Colonie, New York, c. 1920

S B & B R R
STRAWB RR RIDGE PA

183

Photographer unknown
Susquehanna, Bloomsburg
& Berwick Railroad
Train #3 at a station stop
Ridge, Pennsylvania
c. 1890s.

184

Photographer unknown
Quebec Central /
Canadian Pacific Railway
4-6-2 #2600 during a station stop
Lac-Frontière, Quebec, Canada
n.d.

185
—

Photographer unknown
Canadian National Railway
4-6-2 #5591 at speed
Location unknown, n.d.

186
—

Photographer unknown
Southern Pacific Railroad
*Caboose on main line with
freight train approaching*
Location unknown, 1960s.

187
—

(following spread)
Photographer unknown
Delaware & Hudson Railroad
Path leading to roundhouse
Oneonta, New York, after 1921.
(Jim Shaughnessy Collection)

188

Photographer unknown
Railroad unknown
*Railroad tracks in flooded
area or wetlands*
Location unknown
n.d.

189

Photographer unknown
Grand Trunk Railroad
Locomotive #406 and freight train
Location unknown
n.d.

190

Fred Thatcher
Delaware & Hudson Railroad
Locomotive on steel pier with
Fort William Henry Hotel
and Adirondacks in background
Lake George, New York, c. 1912.
(Jim Shaughnessy Collection)

191

David Joslyn?
Southern Pacific Railroad
*Cab forward and rotary
snowplow on Donner Pass*
near Yuba Gap, California
late 1940s–early 1950s.

192–193

—

Photographer unknown
Delaware & Hudson Railroad
*Two photographs depicting
construction of track #3,
"the Low Grade Line"*
near Schenevus, New York
December 27, 1917.
(Jim Shaughnessy Collection)

194

—

Photographer unknown
Delaware & Hudson Railroad
Village view with Washington
branch train tracks and bridge
Granville, New York, 1920s.
(Jim Shaughnessy Collection)

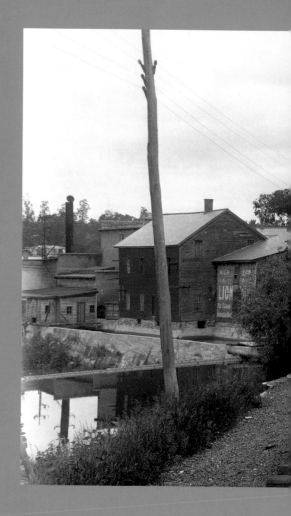

195

—

H. Reid
Strasburg Railroad
2-10-0 #90 with passenger
train in pastoral setting
Strasburg, Pennsylvania
July 28, 1967.

196

—

Photographer unknown
Railroad unknown
Mixed train in bucolic
setting with barn and stream
Location unknown
n.d.

197

—

Photographer unknown
Pennsylvania Railroad
Workers rebuilding boxcars
Terre Haute, Indiana
November 1950.

198

Photographer unknown
Railroad unknown
Railroad workers laying track
with roundhouse in background
Location unknown, n.d.

199

Photographer unknown
Southern Pacific Railroad
Portrait of railroad worker
with shadow of photographer
Oakridge, Oregon, 1950s.
(Wayne Depperman Collection)

200

—

Photographer unknown
Railroad unknown
*Train tracks crossing
small town main street*
Location unknown
n.d.

201

—

Ronald C. Hill
Atchison, Topeka
& Santa Fe Railway
Depot and grain elevators
Oak Hill, Kansas
1963.

202

Photographer unknown
Peoria Union Depot Railroad
Passenger trains under shed
Peoria, Illinois
February 10, 1914.

203

Photographer unknown
Railroad unknown
Portrait of Albany Bridge
Location unknown
n.d.

204

Otto C. Perry
Union Pacific Railroad
4-8-8-4 #4001 leads
westbound freight train,
negative #OP-18451
Riview, Wyoming
November 29, 1941.
(Denver Public Library
Western History Collection)

205

Photographer unknown
Chicago, Rock Island & Pacific Railroad
2-6-6T #1055 in urban setting
Chicago, Illinois, April 15, 1909.

206

Don Ball Jr.
Norfolk & Western Railway
Enginemen check 0-8-0 #284
Location unknown, n.d.

Photographer unknown
Central Pacific Railroad
Enginehouse and settlement
Promontory Summit, Utah?
c. 1890s.

Notes

1. Sarah Greenough, *The Art of the American Snapshot* (Washington, D.C.: National Gallery of Art/Princeton University Press, 2007), 5.

2. Wayne P. Ellis and Herbert H. Harwood Jr., "Ambitious Giant: H. W. Pontin and His Rail Photo Service," *Railroad History* 175 (Autumn 1996), 10–11.

3. Ibid., 16.

4. Ibid., 31.

5. Railway Negative Exchange (REX, also referred to as RNE) was run by Warren Miller who lived in Moraga, California. Born in Oakland in 1923 Miller was this nation's foremost authority on western railroads and devoted virtually his entire life to assembling more than a quarter of a million negatives, most in glass plates, as well as some 200,000 photographs. Upon Miller's death (1989), his collection was left to his nephew Bob Hall.

6. The railroad photographers John Pickett and Jim Shaughnessy remember as teenagers having feelings of being awkward outsiders because of their interest in trains.

7. Freeman Hubbard, "Interesting Railfan no. 100," *Railroad* (April 1971), 27.

8. Arnold S. Menke, "Gerald M. Best's 'Autobiography of a Railfan,' " *Railroad History* 158 (Spring 1988), 23.

9. *Railroad* (November 1935), 115.

10. *Railroad* (September 1937), 138.

11. See http://collectinggoldmagazines.com/magazines/life-magazine/.

12. *Railroad* (February 1972), 33.

13. *Railroad History* 158, 25.

14. Ellis and Harwood, "Ambitious Giant: H. W. Pontin and His Rail Photo Service," 15, 28.

15. Charles Albi and William C. Jones, "Otto C. Perry: A Biographical Sketch," by Richard Kindig, in *Otto Perry: Master Railroad Photographer* (Golden, CO: Colorado Railroad Museum, 1982), 19.

16. *Railroad* (October 1963), 32.

17. *Railroad History* 152 (Spring 1985), 34.

18. Story told to author by Ed Delvers in 1985 concerning the locomotive roster photographs made by Katsusaburo Nishio in Japan during the 1940s.

19. Menke, "Gerald M. Best's 'Autobiography of a Railfan,' " 23.

20. Anne M. Lyden, *Railroad Vision: Photography, Travel and Perception* (Los Angeles: J. Paul Getty Museum, 2003), 9.

21. Lucius Beebe, *Highliners* (New York: Bonanza Books, 1940), ix.

22. George Hilton, "The trains were in transition, and it *was* a fascinating railroad business," *Trains* (November 1990), 82.

23. Albi and Jones, "Otto C. Perry," by Richard Kindig, in *Otto Perry*, 14.

24. Lucius Beebe and Charles Clegg, *Rio Grande: Mainline of the Rockies* (Berkeley, CA: Howell-North Books, 1962), 220–21, 302–3. Perry was also accused of being a German spy while photographing in Union Pacific's Cheyenne yards in 1917, right before being drafted into the army. Perry, for the most part, ended still photography of trains in 1945 when he decided instead to focus almost exclusively on 16mm films of railroad action (with thanks to Charles Albi, railroad historian).

25. Janet Malcolm, *Diana and Nikon: Essays on the Aesthetic of Photography* (Boston: David R. Godine, 1980), 69, quoting Lisette Model.

26. See http://theonlinephotographer.typepad.com/the_online_photographer/2009/03/democratic-vistas-vernacular-photography-and-the-common-man.html.

27. Geoffrey Batchen, "Vernacular Photographies," *History of Photography* 24, no. 3 (Autumn 2000), 262.

28. John A. Kouwenhoven, *Half a Truth Is Better than None* (Chicago: University of Chicago Press, 1982), 80.

29. John Tagg, "A Means of Surveillance," in *The Burden of Representation: Essays on Photographies and Histories* (Minneapolis, MN: University of Minnesota Press, 1988), 97.

30. See *The Photographs of Édouard Baldus* (New York/Montreal: Metropolitan Museum of Art; Canadian Centre for Architecture, 1994).

31. E-mail from David A. Pfeiffer, archivist, Archives II Reference Section (RD-DC), National Archives at College Park, Maryland, September 24, 2012. Contemporary government-sponsored programs such as the Historic Architectural Building Survey (HABS) issue strict guidelines overseeing the photography, film, and print processing of all projects.

32. E-mail from David A. Pfeiffer, archivist, September 24, 2012.

33. See http://www.clevelandmemory.org/wle/index.html.

34. Lyden, *Railroad Vision*, 97.

35. Ibid., 30, 76, 96, 106.

36. Roderick Fraser Nash, *Wilderness and the American Mind*, 4th edition (New Haven, CT: Yale University Press, 2001), 44, 66.

37. See http://www.americanantiquarian.org/stereographs.html.

38. William C. Jones and Elizabeth B. Jones, *Photo by McClure, The Railroad, Cityscape and Landscape Photographs of L. C. McClure* (Boulder, CO: Pruett Publishing, 1983), 1.

39. Peter B. Hales, *William Henry Jackson and the Transformation of the American Landscape* (Philadelphia: Temple University Press, 1988), 156–58.

40. Lyden, *Railroad Vision*, 80.

41. See Luc Sante, *Folk Photography* (Portland, OR: Verse Chorus Press, 2009), 9–37, for an excellent discussion on the history of the postcard.

42. John Szarkowski, *The Photographer's Eye*, 5th edition (New York: Museum of Modern Art, 2012), 8.

208
—
Robert Olmstead
Chicago, Rock Island
& Pacific Railroad
#5106 on freight train
near Lawrence, Kansas
March 13, 1949.

Acknowledgments

The railfan community is a generous one and we've been the lucky recipients of much help and assistance with this project over the past decade. Our network of friends was unfailingly supportive when an inquiry went out for historical information about a photograph's content; their eager responsiveness and cheerful attitudes are amazing. For this we're eternally grateful. We'd like to thank: Shirley Burman, S. R. "Stevie-Luv" Bush, John B. Corns, Wayne Depperman, Mal Farrell, Michael Froio, John Gruber, Victor Hand, Joel Jensen, Scott Lothes, Robert Mohowski, Sheldon Perry, Wayne Sittner, Blake Tater, Jack Swanberg, Rich Taylor, Otto Vondrak and Karl Zimmermann.

While seeking permission to publish images we had the good fortune to become acquainted with a new set of friends. Our heartfelt thanks go out to Fenner Ball, Mr. and Mrs. Russ Colegrove, Alan Furler, Wally Johnson, W. R. McGee, Jeffrey Koeller, Bill McClure, Chuck McIntyre, Edward H. Miller, Robert Olmstead, David Price, and Margaret Ridgeway.

Several institutions also proved quite helpful on the research front: many thanks to Kyle Wyatt and Ellen Haltemann at the California State Railroad Musuem; Laura Katz Smith and Kristin Eshelman at the Thomas Dodd Research Center at the University of Connecticut, Storrs; Eric Huber at the Queens Borough Public Library, Long Island Division; and Coi Drummond-Gehrig and Charles Albi at the Denver Public Library.

Non-railfan friends Robert and Deborah Bull, Craig Krull, Gail Pine, and Susan Wechsler also merit thanks for sharing information on the history of vernacular photography.

Friend George Cook deserves special recognition for granting access to his extensive magazine archive; an afternoon spent in his library was instrumental in shaping *Vernacular*'s text. A special thanks goes to friend Jim Shaughnessy who graciously lent the project not only his own photographs but a stunning array of glass-plate negatives from his collection as well. Jim also aided our research with his vast respository of railroad knowledge. Good buddy John Pickett was forthcoming with a selection of his exceptional railroad photography from the 1940s and '50s; for this we are grateful. Close pals Dawn Freer and Kathryn Clark read the text, offering valuable insight and critique when the essay was in its formative and final stages.

A deep thanks to our international intern, Clara Prioux, who through the wonders of the Internet performed valuable work from France during the production process.

Jim Mairs, Austin O'Driscoll, and Bill Rusin at W. W. Norton as always deserve our deepest thanks for their continuing belief in our efforts; we doubt a better editorial and marketing team exists in the publishing world. It's always a delight and pleasure working with you. Thanks also to Don Kennison.

Arthur Hoener and Robert Bull (again!) provided technical and typographic support at the eleventh hour. You guys are true friends. Glyphs, ligatures, and folios indeed.

We thank our friends and colleagues at the Center for Railroad Photography & Art in Madison, Wisconsin, for the continual inspiration their valuable efforts in the field of railroad photography provide.

Lastly, we'd like to acknowledge the work of every rail photographer represented within. Without their tireless dedication documenting America's railroads the visual record would be significantly less rich.

Additional Photo Credits

Pages 2–3: **H. Reid,** Norfolk & Western Railroad *4-8-2 #110 hauling coal cars through yard scene* Norfolk, Virginia, 1950s.

Pages 4–5: **Photographer unknown,** Railroad unknown, *Excursionists on a break,* Location unknown, n.d.

Page 6: **Otto C. Perry,** Union Pacific Railroad *4-8-2 #7002 and The 49er,* near Echo, Utah, October 23, 1937. (Denver Public Library Western History Collection)

Some Vernacular Railroad Photographs is dedicated to our dear friend Ed Delvers: a man of great curiosity who also took pleasure in the hunt. We miss you beyond measure.

Some Vernacular Railroad Photographs
Copyright © 2013 by Jeff Brouws and Wendy Burton
ISBN 978-0-393-23938-6

Every reasonable effort has been made to identify the photographers whose works appear in this book. Credits are noted with the photographs when we have been successful. Anyone located in the future will be credited in subsequent reprints of the book.

Book design and composition by Jeff Brouws
Photoshop and scanning by Wendy Burton
Sequencing by Wendy Burton

Manufacturing through Asia-Pacific Offset

Library of Congress Cataloging-in-Publication Data

Brouws, Jeffrey T.
Some vernacular railroad photographs / Jeff Brouws & Wendy Burton.
 —First edition.
    pages cm
ISBN 978-0-393-23938-6 (hardcover)
1. Photography of railroads—History—20th century. 2. Railroads Pictorial works. 3. Photograph collections—United States.
I. Burton, Wendy, 1951- II. Title.
TR715.B76 2013
779'.9385--dc23

                  2012045126

W. W. Norton & Company
500 Fifth Avenue, New York, NY 10110
www.wwnorton.com

W. W. Norton & Company Ltd.
Castle House, 75/76 Wells Street, London, WIT 3QT

1 2 3 4 5 6 7 8 9 0